# THE PRAYER

# OF

# JESUS CRUCIFIED

a simple way to go further in prayer

Fr. Lawrence Edward Tucker, S.O.L.T.

**ENROUTE**
Books and Media

En Route Books and Media, LLC
5705 Rhodes Avenue
St. Louis, MO 63109

Cover credit: TJ Burdick

Library of Congress Control Number: 2017947533

Copyright © 2017 Fr. Lawrence Tucker, S.O.L.T.

All rights reserved.

ISBN-10:0-9991143-2-8
ISBN-13:978-0-9991143-2-2

"It is only by the royal road of the Cross that the Christian soul truly enters into supernatural contemplation of the mysteries of faith and lives lovingly and deeply by them."

*The Love of God and the Cross of Jesus*
(Reginald Garrigou-Lagrange, OP)

Fr. Lawrence Edward Tucker, S.O.L.T.

# **DEDICATION**

To the memory of St. John Paul II, who led the Church across "the threshold of hope" into the third millennium of Christianity and who gave us the *Catechism of the Catholic Church* as our guide. He also gave us many new and wonderful saints such as St. Faustina, the "Apostle of Divine Mercy"... and St. Juan Diego, the humble messenger of our Mother's everlasting love... made manifest in Our Lady of Guadalupe.

And we can never forget the great blessing he bestowed upon us when he named Therese of Lisieux a *Doctor of the Church*. The "little flower," having simplified the complex world of spirituality into her delightful and completely accessible "little way" of spiritual childhood, is at work in the Church now... more than ever before!

May St. John Paul II, who by his own example challenged us to go further in prayer, intercede for the Church as she embarks on a mission that meant so much to him... *The New Evangelization!*

Fr. Lawrence Edward Tucker, S.O.L.T.

"The door of our heart can be opened only by that great and definitive word of the love of Christ for us, which is his death on the cross. It is here that the Lord wishes to lead us; within ourselves."

*— Saint John Paul II, Address of His Holiness, John Paul II, to Six Thousand University Students Coming from all over the World to Participate in an International Congress (April 10, 1979)*

# **CONTENTS**

|     | Acknowledgements | i   |
|-----|------------------|-----|
|     | Preface          | iii |
| 1   | Foreword         | xi  |
| 2   | Introduction     | 1   |
| 3   | Context          | 3   |
| 4   | Way              | 7   |
| 5   | Disposition      | 11  |
| 6   | Blessings        | 15  |
| 7   | Attitude         | 19  |
| 8   | Fruits           | 23  |
| 9   | FAQ's            | 27  |
| 10  | About the Author | 29  |

# ACKNOWLEDGEMENTS

First and foremost, I extend heartfelt thanks to my superior, Fr. Gerard Sheehan, S.O.L.T., for his enthusiasm and support for this project. Thanks also go out to Msgr. George P. Graham, J.C.D. and PhD, Religious Studies, for his encouragement and interest in this work.

Many thanks to Andrea and Patrick Walshe, Dr. Blythe Kaufmann, D.D.S., M.D.S. and Dr. Peter Garrity, PhD, Mathematics, for their friendship and generous assistance with this endeavor.

Also, special thanks to Carlos Montes de Oca and Mariangela Zapata Holliday, of Laredo, TX; Enrique Riddle, San Antonio, TX, and his sister, Patricia Galindo, Piedras Negras, Coah., MX, for their invaluable help with the Spanish edition.

Finally, I like to think of St. Therese of the Child Jesus and the Holy Face as the heavenly patroness of this simple way of contemplative prayer. The Little Flower is known as the teacher of *The Little Way* and I believe she would be pleased with the childlike simplicity of *The Prayer of Jesus Crucified*.

Fr. Lawrence Edward Tucker, S.O.L.T.

# **PREFACE**

Fr. Joseph C. Henchey, CSS, STD

The title of Fr. Tucker's book, *The Prayer of Jesus Crucified,* directs our attention to the heart and core of our Christian faith... the way a computer pointer indicates a specific point on the screen. He helps us to zero in on the depth of the mystery which is Christ our Savior and to learn to contemplate more deeply upon him.

In this way, Fr. Tucker's book is in harmony with the recommendations of Vatican II in *Dei Verbum* 8, which taught that for our faith to grow, we believers need to practice contemplative prayer, continue in our study of Scripture, heed the guidance of the Magisterium and learn from our own experiences as we live more and more in the model of Christ.

Hence, as we take up the subject of contemplative prayer with Fr. Tucker, we might first ask the question: What does the expression, the prayer *of* Jesus crucified, mean? It can be understood in several ways. First, we might think of it in light of Jesus' own personal prayers to his Father (that is, in his filial prayer of *The Our Father*), as well as in the light of those he prayed in the archetype of the Suffering Servant of Isaiah 53 (that is, in his prayer in Gethsemane as well as in The Seven Last Words).

Or, we might understand the prayer *of* Jesus crucified as touching on the great mystery of the prayer surrounding Jesus' entire earthly sojourn, and that of the continuing life of the Church.[1]

Jesus' personal prayer (or what we might call his "subjective" prayer) illuminates the Mystery of the Trinity and the fully integrated dimensions of the Redemption in which his entire earthly life, that is, his daily life, death, Passion and Resurrection… all redeem us.[2]

Jesus' archetypic prayer (or what we might call his "objective" prayer) could be considered a reflection on the "Pierced One" which, in the book by Cardinal Ratzinger of the same name, reveals to us that Christ's entire life was encased in prayer. He was born in prayer, lived in prayer, was tempted in prayer and finally *ex-spired* in prayer as he sent out the Holy Spirit, which Luke reveals in the "temple atmosphere" of his Gospel with its emphasis on the *Benedictus, Magnificat* and *Nunc Dimittis*. One might also consider Pope Paul VI's Liturgy of Hours Decree, *Canticum Laudis,* as a way of understanding how the Church continues this prayer of Jesus through the ages.

Indeed, it is a proof of the merciful high priesthood of Jesus that he persevered in prayer all through his life, and he continues to intercede for us, eternally celebrating with Mary and all the angels and saints in the celestial sanctuary. He is indeed… *"a priest forever!"*[3]

Recently, a sublime study on the *Crucified God*, written by the renowned Evangelical theologian, Jurgen Moltmann, has been republished in honor of the 40th anniversary of its writing. While the title might appear to be somewhat at odds with mainstream Catholic teaching, it is in fact quite consistent with St. Thomas Aquinas' own views which he drew from the teaching of St. Cyril at the Council of Ephesus.

St. Thomas wrote: *"Christ's death, being as it were, God's death… namely by union in Person… 'destroyed death'; since he who suffered was both God and man. For God's nature was not wounded, nor did it undergo any change by those sufferings…"*[4] And further he writes, *"…the Passion is to be attributed to the suppositum of the divine nature, not because of the divine nature, which is impassable, but by reason of the human nature…"*[5]

Fr. Tucker's book also draws on a statement by the great early 20th century theologian, Fr. Reginald Garrigou-Lagrange, OP, who wrote: *"St. Thomas made it his special task to lay bare the essence or nature of the infused virtues and of the gifts of the Holy Spirit, reasoning to their properties and mutual relationships and St. John of the Cross has described their progress to perfect development…"* [6]

The prayer of Christ crucified easily brings to mind the "dark night of the soul" experienced by so many saints and which is expressed in the anguished prayer we so often hear in the funeral liturgies called… *De Profundis: "Out of the depths I cry unto you, O Lord!"* [7]

Throughout history, humans have struggled with this "dark night of the soul," which St. John of the Cross described in his book of the same name. For years, St. John expressed his spiritual experience as *"nada"*, meaning *"nothing"* in Spanish. Yet from these depths of "nothingness", we are reminded of the words of the Benedictus: *"By the tender mercy of our God, the dawn from on high will bring the rising sun to give light to those who live in darkness and the shadow of death…"* [8]

Thus, the cross is like Jacob's ladder, leading us out of the confining anguish and hopeless depths of the "dark night" and enabling us to uncover its secret. We cannot forget that the Lord promises: *"When I am raised up (on the cross and in the resurrection) I will draw all to myself."* [9]

By repeating and living the *nada* ourselves, our own self-emptying is modeled on Christ's kenosis. It is contemplative prayer that enables us to *"put on the mind of Christ Jesus… who emptied himself… by his death on the cross."* [10] This self-emptying is a total commitment, as St. Ignatius of Loyola put it, *"for the **ever greater*** *glory of God"...* for only God knows what he would do in the souls of believers were he not impeded by them. For the greater glory of God, St. Francis of Assisi asked his followers to abase themselves, calling them members of the order of *the lesser brothers...* as they lived a most ascetic life.

Indeed, all the baptized are called *"to make of their lives an oblation to the mercy of God."* [11] Emmanuel is God in *communion* with us and the revelation is that Christ is *in* us. This is an eschatological formula meant to last forever.[12] Therefore, we must make room for God by emptying ourselves. In every Eucharist we share in the cross in an unbloody manner. Like the Suffering Servant, our lives are meant to be an Atonement [13] *"...by his wounds, ours are healed"...*because *"he surrendered."*

In the Eucharistic liturgy, the Church prays: *"Lift up your hearts!"* Mary teaches us to do the same as we watch her stand by the cross. We are confident in this hopeful perseverance because we believe the words: *"Once I was dead, but now I live... forever and ever. I hold the keys of death and the nether-world."* [14]

So, let us think of the Eucharist as a *faith* to believe, a *liturgy* to celebrate and a *life* to lead... the way Pope Benedict encourages us to do in *Sacramentum Caritatis.* Jesus was offered up by the Father and was not spared.[15] He was consecrated and sent into this world[16] to be one with us as he is with his Father.[17]

A beautiful Eastern Icon shows the Crucifixion of Christ taking place right on the tomb of Adam and Eve as he calls them forth from the prison of their grave. While the first Good Friday was a date in history, St. Thomas teaches us that, in truth, God is totally outside the order of time, as though constituted in the bulwark (summit, citadel, refuge, abode) *"of eternity to whom lies subject the entire unfolding of time to his one and simple view."* [18] Until our entrance into eternity, the Eucharist feeds our hope because we *"believe in the One who raised Jesus from the dead, who was handed over for our transgressions and was raised for our justification..."* [19]

---

1  For example, the *"Jesus Prayer"*: *"Jesus, Son of God, Mary, have mercy on us!"*

2  Rm 4:25

3  cf. Heb 5:6; 6:20; 7:3, 17, 21, 24, 25, 28.

4  cf. III, q. 46, a. 12, ad 2 um

5  cf. I, q. 16, a. 4 – citation noted by Fr. Cornelio Fabro, CSS, in his study on St. Gemma Galgani, the Witness to the Supernatural.

6  *The Love of God and the Cross of Jesus,* Vol. I  (Fr. Reginald Garrigou-Lagrange, OP)

7  Ps 130

8  Lk 1:78, ff.

9  Jn 12:32

10  Ph 2:5-11

11  cf. Rm 12:1, f.

12  2 Co 3:18; 25: 1-10

13  cf. Is 53: 5, 13

14  Rv 1:17, f.

15  cf. Rm 8:32; Jn 3:16
16  cf. Jn 10: 36
17  cf. Jn 15
18  St. Thomas Aquinas *comm. In Periherm.*, Book I, c. 9, Lectio 14 – text quoted by Fr. Cornelio Fabro, CSS
19 Rm 34: 25

**Icon of Harrowing of Hades, fresco in the parecclesion of the Chora Church, Istanbul, c. 1315**
(Image Source: Wikipedia)

# **FOREWORD**

Prayer is a mysterious thing. On the one hand, nothing should come more naturally to us, for as Saint Augustine famously said, "You have made us for yourself, O Lord, and our hearts are restless until they rest in you." Prayer, converse and communion with God, is a way of resting in him who is our hearts' deepest longing.

On the other hand, because of our fallen human nature, prayer, at least on any deep and significant level, often appears unattainable and, in the frenetically paced world of the internet and social media, even unattractive.

The great merit of Fr. Larry's lovely little book, *The Prayer of Jesus Crucified*, is its combination of simplicity and beauty. The simplicity addresses our doubts about being able to achieve a deeper level of prayer than that to which we may be accustomed, the beauty our suspicion that prayer is likely a cold, lifeless, and tedious enterprise.

Read this little book slowly and thoughtfully. Let it touch your heart. Then let it guide you along the path of love to greater intimacy with the Lord. He gives himself to you. Let Fr. Larry's beautiful little prayer help you to give yourself to him.

As Father remarks, you will not be alone in your effort. The Mother of Jesus, seeing your embrace of her Son, will rush to your side. Your life cannot but be better for being bathed in the light of two such loving companions.

> Msgr. Charles R. Fink,
> former Spiritual Director at
> St. Joseph's Seminary, New York

Cover Image of *Marrying the Rosary to the Divine Mercy Chaplet* by Shane Kapler
(En Route Books and Media, 2016)

## INTRODUCTION

In the *Catechism of the Catholic Church*, the last sentence of paragraph 2708 deals with meditation as a form of prayer: *"This form of prayerful reflection is of great value, but Christian prayer should go further: to the knowledge of the love of the Lord Jesus, to union with him."* Immediately following this sentence, in paragraphs 2709-2719, the Church provides a profoundly beautiful teaching on contemplative prayer.

Many people have the desire to "go further" in prayer… to become one with Jesus in the calm of interior/contemplative prayer; but they have difficulty discovering a suitable way forward.

Since, as the *Catechism* states (2713): *"Contemplative prayer is the simplest expression of the mystery of prayer",* The Prayer of Jesus Crucified describes, in a concise and inspiring manner, a simple way of wordless, silent prayer that is in conformity with the Church's teaching on contemplative prayer. It can help a person "go further" into union with Jesus so that they can say with St. Paul: *"I have been crucified with Christ… and the life I live now is not my own; Jesus is living in me!"* (Galatians 2:20).

While the primary objective of contemplative prayer is union with Jesus… oneness with Jesus takes on a life of its own. Due to the spiritual poverty that is always at the heart of contemplative prayer, the person comes to encounter, perhaps for the first time, the impoverished Jesus and will find themselves being drawn into his mission *"to bring good news to the poor!"* (Lk 4:18).

As Pope Francis points out in Evangelii Gaudium (209), Jesus is *"the evangelizer par excellence and the Gospel in person"* and, *"the best incentive for sharing the Gospel comes from contemplating it with love…" (264)*. One can see, therefore, how fitting it is in this time of *The New Evangelization* for souls to respond to the call to "go further" in prayer, for, as Pope Francis declared in Evangelii Gaudium (262): *The Church urgently needs the deep breath of prayer."*

## **CONTEXT**

JESUS SAID THAT

WHEN HE WAS LIFTED UP (on the cross),

HE WOULD DRAW ALL MEN TO HIMSELF.

HE WAS LIFTED UP, AND SO,

WE ARE DRAWN TO HIM.

THE PRAYER OF JESUS CRUCIFIED

IS A SIMPLE WAY OF ENTERING INTO THIS

MYSTERY OF THE HEART OF JESUS.

Fr. Lawrence Edward Tucker, S.O.L.T.

IT FACILITATES THE DEEP DESIRE
THAT JESUS HAS TO BE ONE WITH US;
TO DRAW US INTO THE DEPTHS OF HIS
HEART, THE MYSTERIES OF HIS PASSION
AND LOVE, THE FULLNESS OF HIS
TRINITARIAN LIFE!

AT THE SAME TIME,
IT FACILITATES OUR INMOST DESIRE
TO BE ONE WITH JESUS,
A PROFOUND LONGING WITHIN US
THAT HAS ITS ORIGIN IN JESUS.

THE MORE WE ALLOW JESUS
TO DRAW US INTO
HIS HEART'S DESIRE FOR SOULS,
HIS ALL CONSUMING
HUNGER AND THIRST FOR US,

THE MORE SPIRITUALIZED WE BECOME.

IN EFFECT,

WE BECOME LIKE HIM...

AFLAME WITH LOVE!

"I have come to set a fire on the earth... how I long to see it kindled!" - Lk 12:49


THIS, THEN, IS OUR JOY!

TO BE ONE WITH OUR LORD JESUS...

TO LIVE IN HIS HEART AND TO SERVE

IN HIS LOVE!

"I give you one command... to love as I have loved" - Jn 15:12


HOW WONDROUS!

JESUS COMMANDS OUR JOY!

HE IS OUR JOY.

Fr. Lawrence Edward Tucker, S.O.L.T.

AND AS WE BECOME ONE WITH HIM

IN HIS WOUNDED AND MERCIFUL HEART,

AGLOW WITH THE WARMTH OF OUR

FATHER'S ETERNAL LOVE,

HE ALSO BECOMES OUR PEACE.

**Sacred Heart at the Centre of a rose window**,
Santa Ifigênia Church, São Paulo, Brazil
(Image source: Wikipedia)

## **WAY**

THE PRAYER OF JESUS CRUCIFIED IS ONE

WAY, A VERY SIMPLE WAY,

OF ENTERING INTO THE SPIRITUAL RIVER

OF PEACE, JOY AND LOVE

THAT FLOWS OUT OF THE DEPTHS OF

THE HEART OF JESUS.

"I will give you living water!" Jn 4:10

THIS PRAYER IS SO SIMPLE THAT,

AT FIRST GLANCE,

Fr. Lawrence Edward Tucker, S.O.L.T.

IT MIGHT SEEM THAT IT IS ONLY SUITABLE
FOR CHILDREN.
AND YET, DID NOT OUR MASTER SAY THAT
UNLESS WE BECOME LIKE CHILDREN,
WE WILL NOT ENTER THE KINGDOM?

AND SO, IN ORDER TO BE *GREAT*
IN THE HEART OF JESUS,
WE MUST BECOME *LITTLE*.
THEREFORE, SINCE JESUS SAID THAT
WHEN HE WAS LIFTED UP HE WOULD
DRAW US, WE LIFT HIM UP!

IN THE PRAYER OF JESUS CRUCIFIED
WE LIFT UP THE CRUCIFIX, KISS IT,
AND HOLD IT AGAINST OUR CHEST,
RIGHT OVER OUR HEART…
IN SUCH A WAY THAT HIS HEART

PIERCED THROUGH WITH LOVE, IS DIRECTLY FACING OUR OWN HEART. BY HOLDING THE CRUCIFIX IN THIS POSITION, THE HEART-TO-HEART CONVERSATION WE LONG TO HAVE WITH JESUS BEGINS, AS WE EMBRACE THE MYSTERY OF CRUCIFIED LOVE… JESUS… MADE ONE WITH US BY BEING NAILED TO A CROSS.

THE SENTIMENTS OF THE SOUL AT THIS POINT ARE VERY MUCH LIKE THOSE OF ST. FAUSTINA, WHO UNDERSTOOD HER HEART AS BEING A DWELLING PLACE FOR JESUS; A SACRED ABODE NO ONE ELSE COULD ENTER... ONLY JESUS!

Fr. Lawrence Edward Tucker, S.O.L.T.

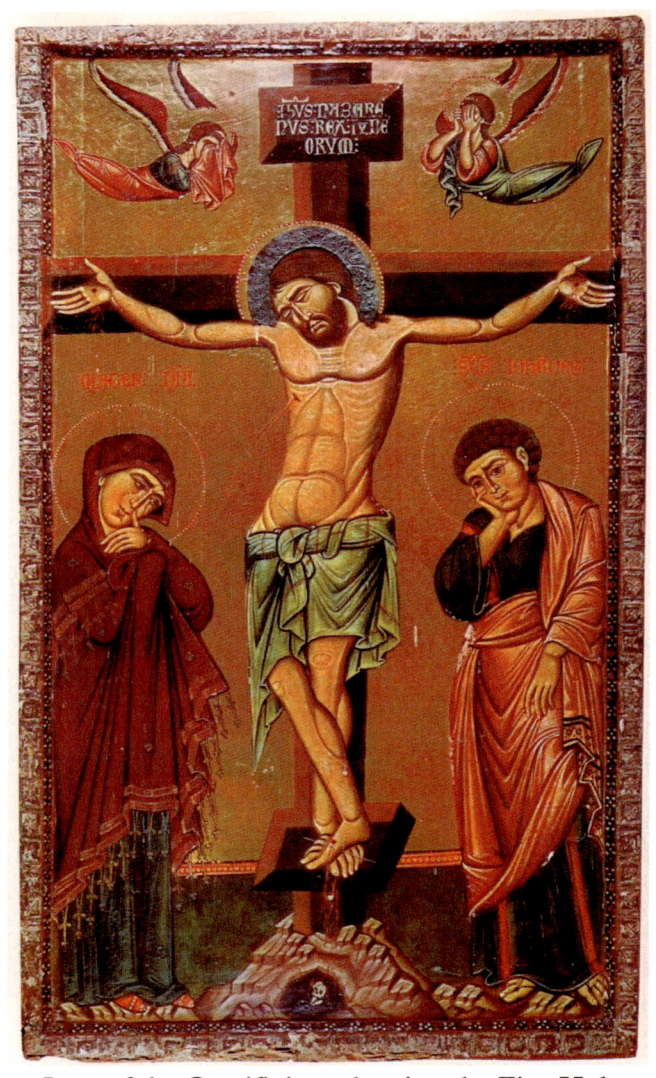

**Icon of the Crucifixion, showing the Five Holy Wounds (13th century, Saint Catherine's Monastery, Mount Sinai)**

(Image Source: Wikipedia)

## **DISPOSITION**

AS THE PRAYER BEGINS,

THE SOUL RECALLS

THAT ALL GOD WANTS TO DO IS LOVE US…

THIS IS HIS GREATEST DESIRE!

HE LIVES WITHIN US AND IS ALWAYS

PRESENT THERE LOVING US.

IN THE PRAYER,

WE RECOGNIZE THIS REALITY

AND ALLOW GOD

TO LOVE US TO HIS HEART'S CONTENT.

AT THE SAME TIME,
THE SOUL RECOGNIZES AND ACCEPTS
ITS TOTAL DEPENDENCE ON
THE LOVE OF GOD…
POURED OUT IN US THROUGH JESUS
CRUCIFIED.

WHEN THE SOUL ACCEPTS THE TRUTH OF
ITS UTTER DEPENDENCE ON
GOD'S LOVE,
THE HEART OPENS AND BLOSSOMS
IN HUMILITY…
COMING TO LIFE IN THE SIMPLICITY OF
GOD'S GIFT OF HIMSELF IN THE HIDDEN
RECESSES OF THE SOUL.
THUS, THE TRUTH
CONCERNING OUR TOTAL DEPENDENCE

ON GOD,

IS COMPLEMENTED BY THE REALITY OF…

HIS EVER PRESENT LOVE

RADIATING WITHIN US!

**Icon of the Holy Trinity
(Andrei Rublev, 1410)**
(Image source: Wikipedia)

## **BLESSINGS**

HAVING DISPOSED ITSELF IN THIS WAY,

AND BEING OPEN TO

THE WONDROUS MYSTERY OF JESUS CRUCIFIED

DRAWING US TO HIMSELF,

THE SOUL IS NOW READY

TO BASK IN GOD'S LOVE,

AND TO ENJOY

ALL THE SUBLIME GIFTS AND BLESSINGS

THAT FLOW FROM
INTIMATE COMMUNION WITH HIM.
THE IDEA HERE IS
TO SIMPLY *BE* WITH GOD…
TO REST IN HIS LOVING PRESENCE
FOR A PERIOD OF TIME.
"Abide in my love!" - Jn 15:9

AS THE PERSON GIVES THIS PRAYER TIME
OVER TO GOD AS A SACRIFICIAL OFFERING
FILLED WITH LOVE, IT SERVES TO
REPRESENT ONE'S ENTIRE LIFE.
CONSEQUENTLY, THE SOUL BEGINS TO
EXPERIENCE THE SACRIFICIAL LOVE OF
JESUS CRUCIFIED.

FOR THIS REASON,
THE PRAYER IS SIMILAR TO…

A SPIRITUAL CRUCIFIXION;

IN THAT,

THE PERSON IS PRESENT BEFORE GOD

AS A LOVING OBLATION.

IT IS LIKE

BEING ON THE CROSS

IN AS MUCH AS

THERE IS NO WHERE TO GO AND

NOTHING TO DO, EXCEPT…TO LOVE!

ALTHOUGH THE SOUL

FINDS ITSELF ON THE CROSS IN THIS

PRAYER, IT DISCOVERS *TRUE* REST

AND A PEACE THE WORLD CANNOT GIVE.

WHAT PURE JOY IT IS

TO EMBRACE JESUS CRUCIFIED!

WE ARE TOLD THAT

Fr. Lawrence Edward Tucker, S.O.L.T.

# ST. FRANCIS OF ASSISI HAD A VISION IN WHICH HE EMBRACED JESUS ON THE CROSS. AND THE HUMBLE "POVERELLO" WAS TRANSFORMED IN LOVE!

**Saint Francis embracing Christ on the Cross (Bartolomé Esteban Murillo, 1668)**
(Image Source: Wikipedia)

## **ATTITUDE**

ONE SHOULD NOT COME TO THIS PRAYER

WITH ANY EXPECTATIONS…

OR BE SEEKING VISIONS OR

CONSOLATIONS.

THE BEAUTY AND POWER OF THIS PRAYER

IS IN ITS VERY SIMPLICITY.

THE SOUL SHOULD BE ANIMATED

BY ONE SIMPLE DESIRE;

Fr. Lawrence Edward Tucker, S.O.L.T.

TO LOSE ITSELF

IN THE MYSTERY OF GOD'S ETERNAL LOVE.

"He who loses himself for my sake…will find himself!" - Mt 10:39

WHEN THE HEART IS FOCUSED

ON THIS ONE SIMPLE DESIRE,

IT BEGINS TO RESEMBLE

THE HEART OF JESUS;

A HEART

SO FILLED WITH LOVE,

THERE WAS NO ROOM

FOR USELESS SELF-SEEKING.

THIS IS

THE TRANSFORMATION IN LOVE

THAT TAKES PLACE

AS JESUS CRUCIFIED DRAWS US TO

HIMSELF.

IN THIS PRAYER

THE EMPHASIS IS ON GIVING,

NOT RECEIVING.

"Father… into your hands I commend my spirit!"

Lk 23:46

THIS IS EVIDENCE OF

THE SPIRITUAL DEPTH OF THIS

TRULY CONTEMPLATIVE PRAYER.

IT DOES NOT DEPEND ON FEELINGS.

IT IS BASED ON THE UNFATHOMABLE
LOVE OF GOD.

**Mosaic of Christ, Haggia Sophia**
(Image source: Wikipedia)

## **FRUITS**

IF A SOUL CONTINUES WITH THIS PRAYER,

DESPITE THE ABSENCE OF

EMOTIONAL EXPERIENCES

AND DRAMATIC SPIRITUAL EVENTS,

A MARVELOUS INTERIOR DEVELOPMENT

WILL BEGIN TO TAKE ROOT.

THE PERSON WILL DISCOVER

A NEW, MYSTICAL WAY

Fr. Lawrence Edward Tucker, S.O.L.T.

OF BEING WITH GOD.

THE SOUL LONGS FOR THIS BEAUTIFUL,

SERENE COMMUNION WITH GOD.

IT WAS CREATED FOR THIS,

AND WHEN IT FINDS THIS

*PEARL OF GREAT PRICE*

ITS JOY IS COMPLETE!

JESUS CRUCIFIED

DRAWS THE SOUL TO HIMSELF

SO THAT HE CAN FILL THE SOUL

WITH HIS OWN ETERNAL LIFE.

AS JESUS POURS

THIS GIFT OF NEW LIFE

INTO THE SOUL,

THE PERSON COMES TO SENSE WHAT LIFE

WAS LIKE IN THE GARDEN OF EDEN.

TO STROLL PEACEFULLY,

IN THE COOL OF THE EVENING,

WITH OUR FATHER.

AMONG THE MANY FRUITS AND BLESSINGS

THAT FLOW

FROM THIS WAY OF PRAYER,

THERE REMAINS ONE THAT IS

TRULY WORTH NOTING.

WHEN JESUS WAS ON THE CROSS,

AT THE HEIGHT OF

HIS AGONY AND PASSION,

HE GAVE US HIS MOTHER

AND TOLD US TO TAKE HER

INTO OUR HEART

AND TO MAKE A HOME FOR HER THERE.

Fr. Lawrence Edward Tucker, S.O.L.T.

OUR MOTHER CANNOT RESIST THE SOUL

THAT STANDS AT THE FOOT OF THE CROSS

AND EMBRACES HER SON,

JESUS CRUCIFIED,

AS SHE HERSELF DID!

SHE WILL RUSH TO THAT SOUL,

TAKE UP RESIDENCE THERE,

AND NEVER LEAVE.

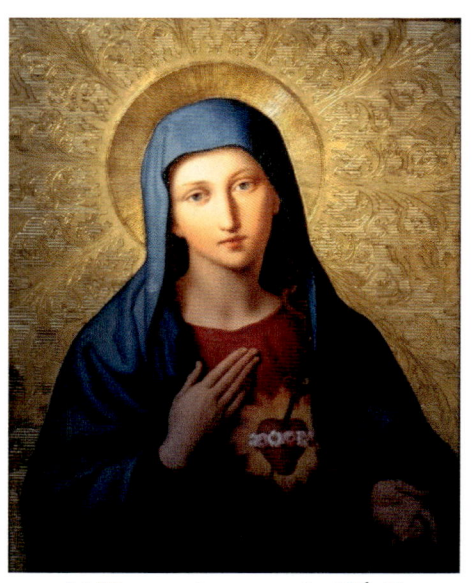

**(Leopold Kuperwieser, early 19th Century)**
(Image Source: Wikipedia)

## **FAQs**

1) How often should I pray this prayer?

   *"One does not undertake contemplative prayer only when one has the time: one makes time for the Lord, with the firm determination not to give up, no matter what trials and dryness one may encounter." Catechism of the Catholic Church* (2710).

The suggestion, therefore, would be once a day. Regarding the duration of the prayer, in general: no less than 5 minutes, and no more than 1 hour.

2) What position should I be in when I pray this prayer?

Choose whatever position in which you are most comfortable.

3) Can this way of prayer be prayed in a group?

Yes. It is no different than any other prayer-form in this respect. When it is prayed in a group, it is helpful if the leader begins by praying aloud psalm 23, and concludes the quiet prayer time by praying aloud our Lady's Magnificat.

4) Where does this particular way of prayer come from?

Contemplative prayer, in general, is an ancient tradition… Jesus and Mary prayed at times without using words. In a context of prayer and inspiration, Fr. Tucker developed *The Prayer of Jesus Crucified* when he was just beginning his priestly life and was searching for a simple, quiet way to pray.

# **ABOUT THE AUTHOR**

Fr. Tucker was born on May 26th, 1955, in Manhattan, New York City. He is a bilingual missionary priest in *The Society of Our Lady of the Most Holy Trinity* and has served in Mexico, Belize, Guatemala, England, Texas, and New York.

Fr. Tucker holds an A.A. in Liberal Arts from Nassau Community College, Garden City, NY; a B.A. from St. Joseph's College, Patchogue, NY; and a Master of Divinity, as well as an M.A. in Theology from Holy Apostles Seminary, Cromwell, CT.